WHAT DOES YOUR DOG DO EVERY DAY?

by Jill Arthur

with illustrations by Jennifer Sauer

A FIRESIDE BOOK
Published by Simon & Schuster
New York   London   Toronto   Sydney   Tokyo   Singapore

F

FIRESIDE
Rockefeller Center
1230 Avenue of the Americas
New York, NY 10020

FIRESIDE and colophon are registered trademarks
of Simon & Schuster Inc.

Designed by Stanley S. Drate/Folio Graphics Co., Inc.

Manufactured in the United States of America

10   9   8   7   6   5   4   3   2   1

Library of Congress Cataloging-in-Publication Data
Arthur, Jill.
    What does your dog do every day? / Jill Arthur : with illustrations by Jennifer Sauer.
       p.   cm.
    "A Fireside book."
    1. Dogs—Humor.   I. Title.
   PN6231.D68A78   1995
818'.5407—dc20
                                                    95-15324
                                                       CIP

ISBN 0-684-80044-6

For Lucy and Levi
    Frau and Charlie

Thank you to Mom and Dad for getting me my first dachshund and making me believe that I could do anything.

Thank you to Jacki for being my best friend and the best sister in the world.

Thank you to all my friends and family (you know who you are), who have always been so supportive.

Thank you to Jennifer Sauer for bringing my words to life.

Of course I want to thank my agents at William Morris—Mike Sheresky and the wonderful Marcy Posner—for loving my book!

And special thanks to my amazing editor, Betsy Radin (and the awesome Fletch), who is beyond the best.

People always ask me

"What does your dog do every day?"

I always answer

Once a week he does the laundry

and folds it.

He does the ironing

and picks up the dry cleaning.

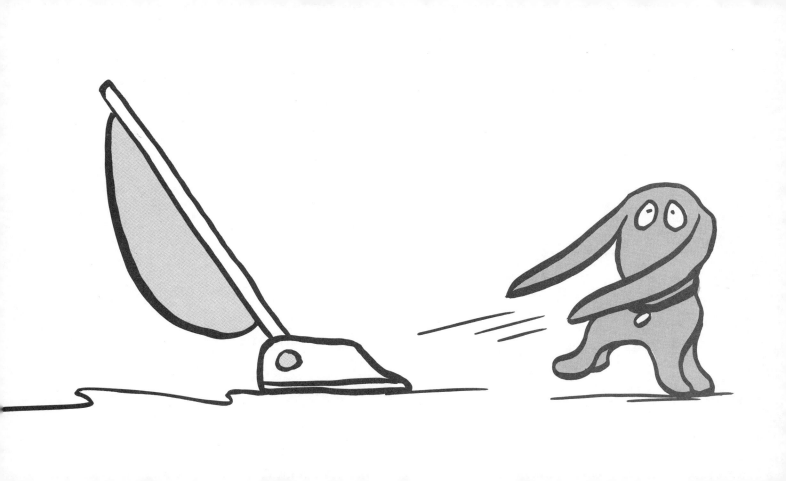

and mop the floors.

He washes the windows

does the dusting

and makes the bed.

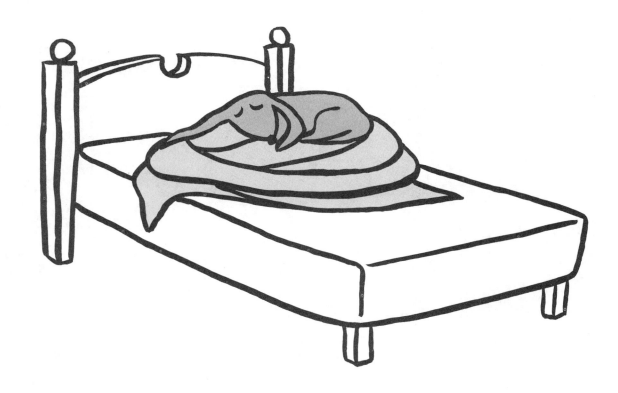

When there's time, he fixes dinner

clears the table

and does the dishes.

To be extra nice to me, he cleans out the refrigerator.

I often ask him to take out the trash

and do the recycling.

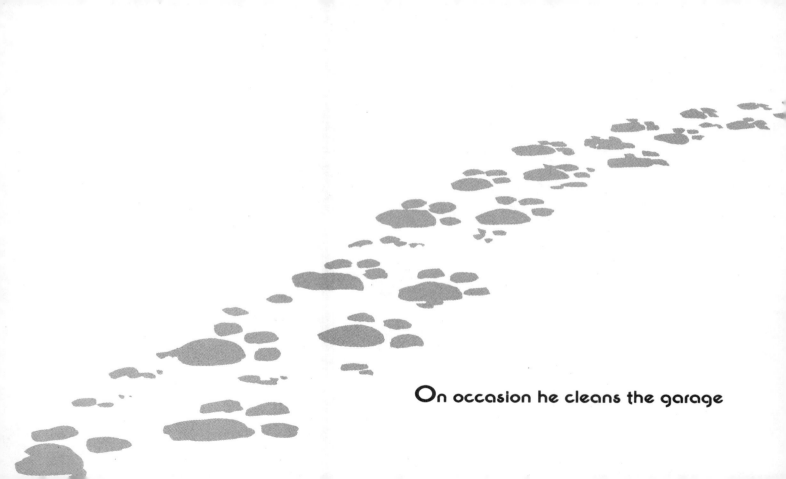

On occasion he cleans the garage

and organizes the closets.

He touches up the paint around the house

and always remembers to water the plants

do the gardening

and arrange the flowers.

He keeps fit by using the exercise equipment

and the electric company.

He's great at taking phone messages

getting the mail

and balancing the checkbook.

He even gets to those books I never can get to

sneaks in videos I haven't had time to watch

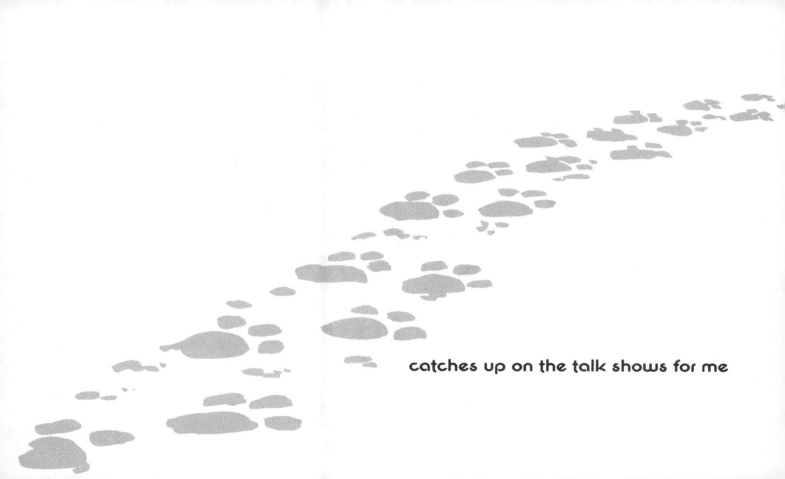

catches up on the talk shows for me

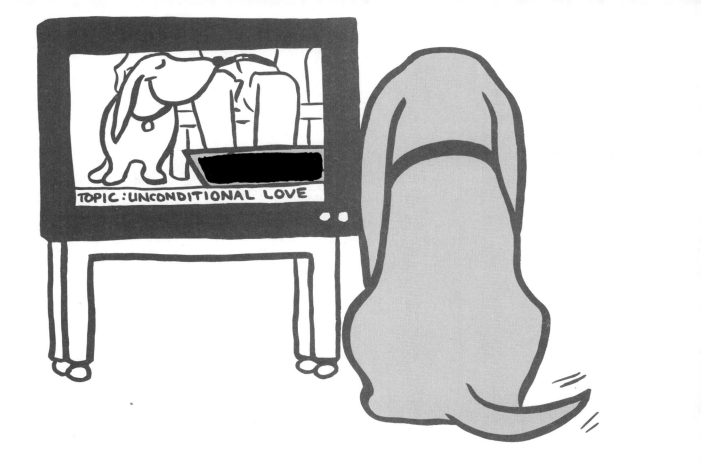

and lets me know who's new on the music scene.

He keeps me up-to-date on the hot news stories

and is learning to speak a foreign language.

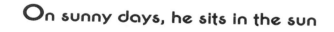

On sunny days, he sits in the sun

or goes for a swim in the yard.

When he's good, he takes a bath

and brushes his teeth.

He takes care of the cat for me

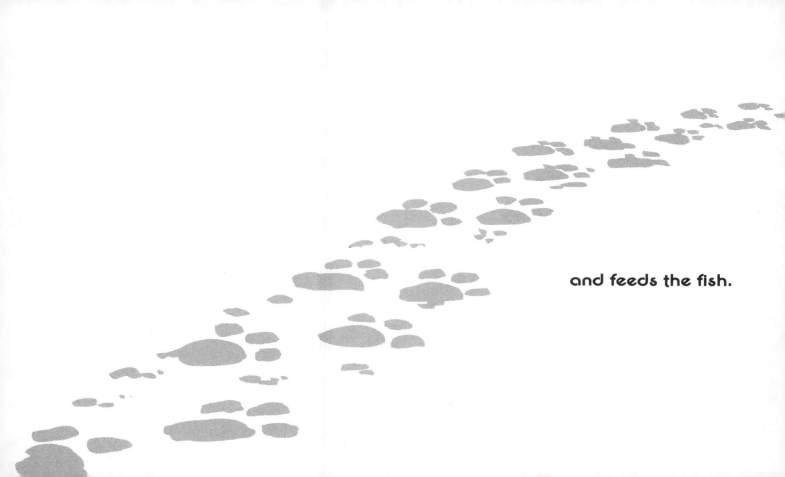

and feeds the fish.

Sometimes he invites his friends over for a bite to eat.

I shouldn't forget to mention that he protects the house all day from unwanted visitors.

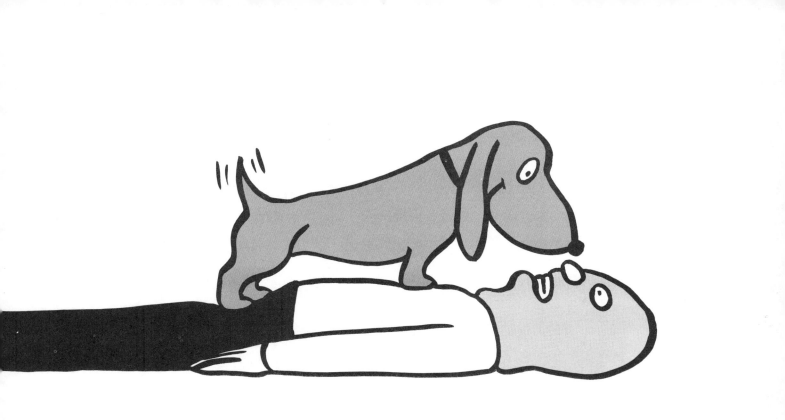

Best of all . . . at the end of every day,
he's there for me when I come home.